**CONVENTION BETWEEN
THE UNITED STATES OF AMERICA
AND THE REPUBLIC OF POLAND
FOR THE AVOIDANCE OF DOUBLE TAXATION AND THE
PREVENTION OF FISCAL EVASION
WITH RESPECT TO TAXES ON INCOME**

The United States of America and the Republic of Poland, desiring to conclude a Convention for the avoidance of double taxation and the prevention of fiscal evasion with respect to taxes on income, have agreed as follows:

Article 1
GENERAL SCOPE

1.   This Convention shall apply only to persons who are residents of one or both of the Contracting States, except as otherwise provided in the Convention.

2.   This Convention shall not restrict in any manner any benefit now or hereafter accorded:

      a)   by the laws of either Contracting State; or

      b)   by any other agreement to which both Contracting States are parties.

3.   a)   Notwithstanding the provisions of subparagraph b) of paragraph 2 of this Article:

            i)   for purposes of paragraph 3 of Article XXII (Consultation) of the General Agreement on Trade in Services (GATS), the Contracting States agree that any question arising as to the interpretation or application of this Convention and, in particular, whether a taxation measure is within the scope of this Convention, shall be determined exclusively in accordance with the provisions of Article 25 (Mutual Agreement Procedure) of this Convention; and

            ii)   the provisions of Article XVII of the General Agreement on Trade in Services (GATS) shall not apply to a taxation measure unless the competent authorities agree that the measure is not within the scope of Article 24 (Non-Discrimination) of this Convention.

      b)   For the purposes of this paragraph, a "measure" is a law, regulation, rule, procedure, decision, administrative action, or any similar provision or action.

4.   Notwithstanding the provisions of paragraph 2, and except to the extent provided in paragraph 5, this Convention shall not affect the taxation by a Contracting State of its residents (as determined under Article 4 (Resident)) and its citizens. Notwithstanding the other provisions of this Convention, a former citizen or former long-term resident of a Contracting State may, for the period of ten years following the loss of such status, be taxed in accordance with the laws of that Contracting State, but only on income from sources within

that Contracting State (including income deemed to arise from sources within that Contracting State under the domestic law of that Contracting State).

5.   The provisions of paragraph 4 shall not affect:

a)   the benefits conferred by a Contracting State under paragraph 2 of Article 9 (Associated Enterprises), paragraphs 2, 3 and 5 of Article 18 (Pensions, Social Security, Annuities, Alimony, and Child Support), and Articles 23 (Elimination of Double Taxation), 24 (Non-Discrimination), and 25 (Mutual Agreement Procedure); and

b)   the benefits conferred by a Contracting State under Articles 19 (Government Service), 20 (Students and Trainees), and 27 (Members of Diplomatic Missions and Consular Posts), upon individuals who are neither citizens of, nor have been admitted for permanent residence in, that State.

6.   a)   Except as provided in subparagraph b), an item of income, profit or gain derived through an entity that is fiscally transparent under the laws of either Contracting State shall be considered to be derived by a resident of a Contracting State to the extent that the item is treated for purposes of the taxation law of such Contracting State as the income, profit or gain of a resident.

b)   Subparagraph a) shall not apply to an item of income, profit or gain if the entity described in subparagraph a) is not fiscally transparent under the laws of the State in which the income, profit or gain arises, is organized in a third state, and is eligible for benefits under a convention for the avoidance of double taxation between the third state and the State in which the income, profit or gain arises with respect to that item of income, profit or gain that are more favorable than the benefits provided by the provisions of this Convention with respect to that item.

Article 2
TAXES COVERED

1.   This Convention shall apply to taxes on income imposed by a Contracting State irrespective of the manner in which they are levied.

2.   There shall be regarded as taxes on income all taxes imposed on total income, or on elements of income, including taxes on gains from the alienation of property.

3.   The existing taxes to which this Convention shall apply are:

    a)   in the case of Poland:

        i)   the personal income tax, and

        ii)   the corporate income tax,

(hereinafter referred to as "Polish tax");

    b)   in the case of the United States:

        i)   the Federal income taxes imposed by the Internal Revenue Code (but excluding social security and unemployment taxes), and

        ii)   the taxes imposed with respect to private foundations under sections 4940 through 4948 of the Internal Revenue Code,

(hereinafter referred to as "United States tax").

4.   This Convention shall apply also to any identical or substantially similar taxes that are imposed after the date of signature of the Convention in addition to, or in place of, the existing taxes. The competent authorities of the Contracting States shall notify each other of any significant changes that have been made in their taxation laws.

Article 3
GENERAL DEFINITIONS

1.   For the purposes of this Convention, unless the context otherwise requires:

    a)   the term "person" includes an individual, an estate, a trust, a partnership, a company, and any other body of persons;

    b)   the term "company" means any body corporate or any entity that is treated as a body corporate for tax purposes according to the laws of the state in which it is organized;

c)   the terms "enterprise of a Contracting State" and "enterprise of the other Contracting State" mean respectively an enterprise carried on by a resident of a Contracting State, and an enterprise carried on by a resident of the other Contracting State; the terms also include an enterprise carried on by a resident of a Contracting State through an entity that is treated as fiscally transparent in that Contracting State;

d)   the term "enterprise" applies to the carrying on of any business;

e)   the term "business" includes the performance of professional services and of other activities of an independent character;

f)   the term "international traffic" means any transport by a ship or aircraft, except when such transport is solely between places in a Contracting State;

g)   the term "competent authority" means:

    i)   in the case of Poland, the Minister of Finance or his authorized representative; and

    ii)   in the case of the United States, the Secretary of the Treasury or his delegate;

h)   the term "Poland" means the Republic of Poland, including the territorial sea thereof and any area outside the territorial sea of the Republic of Poland designated under its laws and in accordance with international law as an area within which the sovereign rights of the Republic of Poland with respect to the sea bed and sub-soil and their natural resources may be exercised;

i)   the term "United States" means the United States of America, and includes the states thereof and the District of Columbia; such term also includes the territorial sea thereof and the sea bed and subsoil of the submarine areas adjacent to that territorial sea, over which the United States may exercise sovereign rights in accordance with international law; the term, however, does not include Puerto Rico, the Virgin Islands, Guam or any other United States possession or territory;

j)   the term "national" of a Contracting State means:

    i)   any individual possessing the nationality or citizenship of that State; and

ii)   any legal person, partnership or association deriving its status as such from the laws in force in that State;

k)   the term "pension fund" means any person established in a Contracting State that is:

i)   generally exempt from income taxation in that State; and

ii)   operated principally either:

A)   to administer or provide pension or retirement benefits; or

B)   to earn income for the benefit of one or more persons described in clause A);

l)   the terms "a Contracting State" and "the other Contracting State" mean the United States or the Republic of Poland, as the context requires.

2.   As regards the application of this Convention at any time by a Contracting State, any term not defined therein shall, unless the context otherwise requires, have the meaning that it has at that time under the laws of that State for the purposes of the taxes to which this Convention applies, any meaning under the applicable tax laws of that State prevailing over a meaning given to the term under other laws of that State.

Article 4
RESIDENT

1.   For the purposes of this Convention, the term "resident of a Contracting State" means any person who, under the laws of that State, is liable to tax therein by reason of his domicile, residence, citizenship, place of management, place of incorporation, or any other criterion of a similar nature, and also includes that Contracting State and any political subdivision or local and governmental authority thereof. This term, however, does not include any person who is liable to tax in that State in respect only of income from sources in that State or of profits attributable to a permanent establishment in that State.

2.   The term "resident of a Contracting State" includes:

a)   a pension fund established in that State; and

b)   an organization that is established and maintained in that State exclusively for religious, charitable, scientific, artistic, cultural, or educational purposes,

notwithstanding that all or part of its income or gains may be exempt from tax under the domestic law of that State.

3.   Where, by reason of the provisions of paragraph 1, an individual is a resident of both Contracting States, then his status shall be determined as follows:

a)   he shall be deemed to be a resident only of the State in which he has a permanent home available to him; if he has a permanent home available to him in both States, he shall be deemed to be a resident only of the State with which his personal and economic relations are closer (center of vital interests);

b)   if the State in which he has his center of vital interests cannot be determined, or if he does not have a permanent home available to him in either State, he shall be deemed to be a resident only of the State in which he has an habitual abode;

c)   if he has an habitual abode in both States or in neither of them, he shall be deemed to be a resident only of the State of which he is a national;

d)   if he is a national of both States or of neither of them, the competent authorities of the Contracting States shall endeavor to settle the question by mutual agreement.

4.   Where by reason of the provisions of paragraph 1 a company is a resident of both Contracting States, then if it is created or organized under the laws of one of the Contracting States or a political subdivision thereof, but not under the laws of the other Contracting State or a political subdivision thereof, such company shall be deemed to be a resident only of the first-mentioned Contracting State.

5.   Where by reason of the provisions of paragraphs 1, 2 or 4 a person other than an individual is a resident of both Contracting States, the competent authorities of the Contracting States may by mutual agreement endeavor to determine the mode of application of this Convention to that person.

Article 5
PERMANENT ESTABLISHMENT

1.   For the purposes of this Convention, the term "permanent establishment" means a fixed place of business through which the business of an enterprise is wholly or partly carried on.

2.   The term "permanent establishment" includes especially:

     a)   a place of management;

     b)   a branch;

     c)   an office;

     d)   a factory;

     e)   a workshop; and

     f)   a mine, an oil or gas well, a quarry, or any other place of extraction of natural resources.

3.   A building site, construction, assembly or installation project, or an installation or drilling rig or ship used for the exploration of natural resources, constitutes a permanent establishment only if it lasts, or the exploration activity continues for more than twelve months.

4.   Notwithstanding the preceding provisions of this Article, the term "permanent establishment" shall be deemed not to include:

     a)   the use of facilities solely for the purpose of storage, display or delivery of goods or merchandise belonging to the enterprise;

     b)   the maintenance of a stock of goods or merchandise belonging to the enterprise solely for the purpose of storage, display or delivery;

     c)   the maintenance of a stock of goods or merchandise belonging to the enterprise solely for the purpose of processing by another enterprise;

d)   the maintenance of a fixed place of business solely for the purpose of purchasing goods or merchandise, or of collecting information, for the enterprise;

e)   the maintenance of a fixed place of business solely for the purpose of carrying on, for the enterprise, any other activity of a preparatory or auxiliary character;

f)   the maintenance of a fixed place of business solely for any combination of the activities mentioned in subparagraphs a) through e), provided that the overall activity of the fixed place of business resulting from this combination is of a preparatory or auxiliary character.

5.   Notwithstanding the provisions of paragraphs 1 and 2, where a person - other than an agent of an independent status to whom paragraph 6 applies - is acting on behalf of an enterprise and has and habitually exercises in a Contracting State an authority to conclude contracts on behalf of the enterprise, that enterprise shall be deemed to have a permanent establishment in that State in respect of any activities that the person undertakes for the enterprise, unless the activities of such person are limited to those mentioned in paragraph 4 that, if exercised through a fixed place of business, would not make this fixed place of business a permanent establishment under the provisions of that paragraph.

6.   An enterprise shall not be deemed to have a permanent establishment in a Contracting State merely because it carries on business in that State through a broker, general commission agent, or any other agent of an independent status, provided that such persons are acting in the ordinary course of their business.

7.   The fact that a company that is a resident of a Contracting State controls or is controlled by a company that is a resident of the other Contracting State, or that carries on business in that other State (whether through a permanent establishment or otherwise), shall not be taken into account in determining whether either company has a permanent establishment in that other State.

Article 6
INCOME FROM REAL PROPERTY

1.   Income derived by a resident of a Contracting State from real property including income from agriculture or forestry, situated in the other Contracting State may be taxed in that other State.

2.   The term "real property" shall have the meaning which it has under the law of the Contracting State in which the property in question is situated. The term shall in any case include property accessory to real property (including livestock and equipment used in agriculture and forestry), rights to which the provisions of general law respecting landed property apply, usufruct of real property and rights to variable or fixed payments as consideration for the working of, or the right to work, mineral deposits, sources and other natural resources. Ships and aircraft shall not be regarded as real property.

3.   The provisions of paragraph 1 shall apply to income derived from the direct use, letting, or use in any other form of real property.

4.   The provisions of paragraphs 1 and 3 shall also apply to the income from real property of an enterprise.

Article 7
BUSINESS PROFITS

1.   Profits of an enterprise of a Contracting State shall be taxable only in that State unless the enterprise carries on business in the other Contracting State through a permanent establishment situated therein. If the enterprise carries on business as aforesaid, the profits that are attributable to the permanent establishment in accordance with the provisions of paragraph 2 may be taxed in that other State.

2.   For the purposes of this Article, the profits that are attributable in each Contracting State to the permanent establishment referred to in paragraph 1 are the profits it might be expected to make, in particular in its dealings with other parts of the enterprise, if it were a separate and independent enterprise engaged in the same or similar activities under the same or similar conditions, taking into account the functions performed, assets used and risks assumed by the enterprise through the permanent establishment and through the other parts of the enterprise.

3.   Where, in accordance with paragraph 2, a Contracting State adjusts the profits that are attributable to a permanent establishment of an enterprise of one of the Contracting States and taxes accordingly profits of the enterprise that have been charged to tax in the other State, the other Contracting State shall, to the extent necessary to eliminate double taxation, make an appropriate adjustment if it agrees with the adjustment made by the first-mentioned State; if the other Contracting State does not so agree, the Contracting States shall eliminate any double taxation resulting therefrom by mutual agreement.

4.   Where profits include items of income which are dealt with separately in other Articles of this Convention, then the provisions of those Articles shall not be affected by the provisions of this Article.

5.   In applying this Article, paragraph 6 of Article 10 (Dividends), paragraph 6 of Article 11 (Interest), paragraph 4 of Article 13 (Royalties), paragraph 4 of Article 14 (Capital Gains) and paragraph 2 of Article 21 (Other Income), any income or gain attributable to a permanent establishment during its existence is taxable in the Contracting State where such permanent establishment is situated even if the payments are deferred until such permanent establishment has ceased to exist.

Article 8
SHIPPING AND AIR TRANSPORT

1.   Profits of an enterprise of a Contracting State from the operation of ships or aircraft in international traffic shall be taxable only in that State.

2.   For purposes of this Article, profits from the operation of ships or aircraft include, but are not limited to:

    a)   profits from the rental of ships or aircraft on a full basis;

    b)   profits from the rental on a bareboat basis of ships or aircraft if the rental income is incidental to profits from the operation of ships or aircraft in international traffic; and

    c)   profits from the rental on a bareboat basis of ships or aircraft if such ships or aircraft are operated in international traffic by the lessee.

Profits derived by an enterprise from the inland transport of property or passengers within either Contracting State shall be treated as profits from the operation of ships or aircraft in international traffic if such transport is undertaken as part of international traffic.

3.   Profits of an enterprise of a Contracting State from the use, maintenance, or rental of containers (including trailers, barges, and related equipment for the transport of containers) shall be taxable only in that Contracting State, where such use, maintenance or rental, as the case may be, is incidental to the operation of ships or aircraft in international traffic.

4. The provisions of paragraph 1 shall also apply to the proportionate share of profits from the participation in a pool, a joint business, or an international operating agency.

Article 9
ASSOCIATED ENTERPRISES

1. Where:

a) an enterprise of a Contracting State participates directly or indirectly in the management, control or capital of an enterprise of the other Contracting State; or

b) the same persons participate directly or indirectly in the management, control or capital of an enterprise of a Contracting State and an enterprise of the other Contracting State,

and in either case conditions are made or imposed between the two enterprises in their commercial or financial relations that differ from those that would be made between independent enterprises, then any profits that, but for those conditions, would have accrued to one of the enterprises, but by reason of those conditions have not so accrued, may be included by a Contracting State in the profits of that enterprise and taxed accordingly.

2. Where a Contracting State includes in the profits of an enterprise of that State, and taxes accordingly, profits on which an enterprise of the other Contracting State has been charged to tax in that other State, and the other Contracting State agrees that the profits so included are profits that would have accrued to the enterprise of the first-mentioned State if the conditions made between the two enterprises had been those that would have been made between independent enterprises, then that other State shall make an appropriate adjustment to the amount of the tax charged therein on those profits. In determining such adjustment, due regard shall be had to the other provisions of this Convention and the competent authorities of the Contracting States shall if necessary consult each other.

Article 10
DIVIDENDS

1. Dividends paid by a company that is a resident of a Contracting State to a resident of the other Contracting State may be taxed in that other State.

2.   However, such dividends may also be taxed in the Contracting State of which the company paying the dividends is a resident and according to the laws of that State, but if the beneficial owner of the dividends is a resident of the other Contracting State, except as otherwise provided, the tax so charged shall not exceed:

    a)   5 percent of the gross amount of the dividends if the beneficial owner is a company that owns directly at least 10 percent of the voting stock of the company paying the dividends;

    b)   15 percent of the gross amount of the dividends in all other cases.

This paragraph shall not affect the taxation of the company in respect of the profits out of which the dividends are paid.

3.   Notwithstanding the provisions of paragraph 2, dividends shall not be taxed in the Contracting State of which the company paying the dividends is a resident if:

    a)   the beneficial owner of the dividends is a pension fund that is a resident of the other Contracting State; and

    b)   such dividends are not derived from carrying on of a trade or business by the pension fund or through an associated enterprise.

4.   a)   Subparagraph a) of paragraph 2 shall not apply in the case of dividends paid by a U.S. Regulated Investment Company (RIC) or a U.S. Real Estate Investment Trust (REIT). In the case of dividends paid by a RIC, subparagraph b) of paragraph 2 and paragraph 3 shall apply. In the case of dividends paid by a REIT, subparagraph b) of paragraph 2 and paragraph 3 shall apply only if:

        i)   the beneficial owner of the dividends is an individual or pension fund, in either case holding an interest of not more than 10 percent in the REIT;

        ii)   the dividends are paid with respect to a class of stock that is publicly traded and the beneficial owner of the dividends is a person holding an interest of not more than 5 percent of any class of the REIT's stock; or

        iii)   the beneficial owner of the dividends is a person holding an interest of not more than 10 percent in the REIT and the REIT is diversified.

b)   For purposes of this paragraph, a REIT shall be "diversified" if the value of no single interest in real property exceeds 10 percent of its total interests in real property. For the purposes of this rule, foreclosure property shall not be considered an interest in real property. Where a REIT holds an interest in a partnership, it shall be treated as owning directly a proportion of the partnership's interests in real property corresponding to its interest in the partnership.

c)   The rules of this paragraph shall also apply to dividends paid by companies resident in Poland that the competent authorities have determined by mutual agreement are similar to the United States companies referred to in this paragraph.

5.   For purposes of this Article, the term "dividends" means income from shares or other rights, not being debt-claims, participating in profits, as well as income from other corporate rights that is subjected to the same taxation treatment as income from shares under the laws of the State of which the payer is a resident.

6.   The provisions of paragraphs 2 through 3 shall not apply if the beneficial owner of the dividends, being a resident of a Contracting State, carries on business in the other Contracting State, of which the company paying the dividends is a resident, through a permanent establishment situated therein, and the holding in respect of which the dividends are paid is effectively connected with such permanent establishment. In such case the provisions of Article 7 (Business Profits) shall apply.

7.   A Contracting State may not impose any tax on dividends paid by a resident of the other State, except insofar as the dividends are paid to a resident of the first-mentioned State or the dividends are attributable to a permanent establishment situated therein, nor may it impose tax on a corporation's undistributed profits, except as provided in paragraph 1 of Article 12 (Branch Profits), even if the dividends paid or the undistributed profits consist wholly or partly of profits or income arising in that State.

Article 11
INTEREST

1.   Interest arising in a Contracting State and paid to a resident of the other Contracting State may be taxed in that other State.

2.   However, such interest may also be taxed in the Contracting State in which it arises and according to the laws of that State, but if the beneficial owner of the interest is a resident of

the other Contracting State, the tax so charged shall not exceed 5 percent of the gross amount of the interest.

3.   Notwithstanding the provisions of paragraph 2, interest described in paragraph 1 shall be taxable only in the Contracting State in which the recipient is a resident if the beneficial owner of the interest is a resident of that State, and:

    a)   is that Contracting State or the central bank, a political subdivision, local authority or statutory body thereof;

    b)   the interest is paid by the Contracting State in which the interest arises or by the central bank, a political subdivision, local authority or statutory body thereof;

    c)   the interest is paid in respect of a loan, debt-claim or credit that is owed to, or made, provided, guaranteed or insured by, that Contracting State or a political subdivision, local authority, statutory body or export financing agency thereof;

    d)   is a pension fund, but only if the pension fund does not derive the interest from the carrying on of a business, directly or indirectly; or

    e)   is either:

        i)   a bank;

        ii)   an insurance company; or

        iii)   an enterprise that is unrelated to the payer of the interest, and that substantially derives its gross income from the active and regular conduct of a lending or finance business (other than a bank within the meaning of clause i) of this subparagraph). For purposes of this subparagraph e) iii), the term "lending or finance business" includes the business of:

            A)   making loans;

            B)   purchasing or discounting accounts receivable, notes, or installment obligations;

            C)   engaging in finance leasing (including purchasing, servicing, and disposing of finance leases and related leased assets);

D)   issuing letters of credit or providing guarantees; or

E)   providing charge and credit card services.

4.   Notwithstanding the provisions of paragraphs 2 and 3:

a)   interest paid by a resident of a Contracting State and that is determined with reference to receipts, sales, income, profits or other cash flow of the debtor or a person related to the debtor, to any change in the value of any property of the debtor or a person related to the debtor or to any dividend, partnership distribution or similar payment made by the debtor or a person related to the debtor, and paid to a resident of the other Contracting State also may be taxed in the Contracting State in which it arises, and according to the laws of that State, but if the beneficial owner is a resident of the other Contracting State, the gross amount of the interest may be taxed at a rate not exceeding 15 percent; and

b)   a Contracting State may tax, in accordance with its domestic law, interest accrued with respect to the ownership interests in an arrangement used for the securitization of real estate mortgages or other assets, to the extent that the amount of the interest accrued exceeds the return on comparable debt instruments as specified by the domestic law of that State.

5.   The term "interest" as used in this Article means income from debt claims of every kind, whether or not secured by mortgage, and whether or not carrying a right to participate in the debtor's profits, and in particular, income from government securities and income from bonds or debentures, including premiums or prizes attaching to such securities, bonds or debentures, as well as all other income which, under the taxation law of the Contracting State in which the income arises, is assimilated to income from money lent. Income dealt with in Article 10 (Dividends) and penalty charges for late payment shall not be regarded as interest for the purposes of this Convention.

6.   The provisions of paragraphs 1, 2 and 3 shall not apply if the beneficial owner of the interest, being a resident of a Contracting State, carries on business in the other Contracting State, in which the interest arises, through a permanent establishment situated therein, and the debt-claim in respect of which the interest is paid is effectively connected with such permanent establishment. In such case the provisions of Article 7 (Business Profits) shall apply.

7.   Interest shall be deemed to arise in a Contracting State when the payer is a resident of that State. Where, however, the person paying the interest, whether he is a resident of a Contracting State or not, has in a Contracting State a permanent establishment in connection with which the indebtedness on which the interest is paid was incurred, and such interest is borne by such permanent establishment, then such interest shall be deemed to arise in the State in which the permanent establishment is situated.

8.   Where, by reason of a special relationship between the payer and the beneficial owner or between both of them and some other person, the amount of the interest, having regard to the debt-claim for which it is paid, exceeds the amount which would have been agreed upon by the payer and the beneficial owner in the absence of such relationship, the provisions of this Article shall apply only to the last-mentioned amount. In such case the excess part of the payments shall remain taxable according to the laws of each Contracting State, due regard being had to the other provisions of this Convention.

Article 12
BRANCH PROFITS

1.   a)   A company that is a resident of one of the Contracting States and that has a permanent establishment in the other Contracting State or that is subject to tax in that other State on a net basis on its income that may be taxed in that other State under Article 6 (Income from Real Property) or under paragraph 1 of Article 14 (Capital Gains) may be subject in that other State to a tax in addition to the tax allowable under the other provisions of this Convention.

        b)   Such tax, however, may be imposed:

                i)   on only the portion of the business profits of the company attributable to the permanent establishment and the portion of the income referred to in subparagraph a) that is subject to tax under Article 6 or under paragraph 1 of Article 14 that, in the case of the United States, represents the dividend equivalent amount of such profits or income and, in the case of Poland, is an amount that is analogous to the dividend equivalent amount; and

                ii)   at a rate not in excess of the rate specified in paragraph 2 a) of Article 10 (Dividends).

2.   The excess, if any, of the amount of interest allocable to the profits of a company resident in a Contracting State that are:

a)   attributable to a permanent establishment in the other Contracting State (including gains under paragraph 4 of Article 14); or

b)   subject to tax in the other Contracting State under Article 6 or paragraph 1 of Article 14,

over the interest paid on indebtedness related to that permanent establishment, or in the case of profits subject to tax under Article 6 or paragraph 1 of Article 14, over the interest paid on indebtedness related to that trade or business in that State shall be deemed to arise in that State and be beneficially owned by a resident of the first-mentioned State. The tax imposed under this Article on such interest shall not exceed the applicable rates provided in paragraph 2 of Article 11 (Interest).

Article 13
ROYALTIES

1.   Royalties arising in a Contracting State and paid to a resident of the other Contracting State may be taxed in that other State.

2.   However, such royalties may also be taxed in the Contracting State in which it arises and according to the laws of that State, but if the beneficial owner of the royalties is a resident of the other Contracting State, the tax so charged shall not exceed 5 percent of the gross amount of the royalties.

3.   The term "royalties" as used in this Article means:

a)   payments of any kind received as a consideration for the use of, or the right to use, any copyright of literary, artistic, scientific or other work (including cinematographic films or radio or television broadcasting tapes), any patent, trademark, design or model, plan, secret formula or process, or for information concerning industrial, commercial or scientific experience;

b)   gain derived from the alienation of any property described in subparagraph a), to the extent that such gain is contingent on the productivity, use, or disposition of the property; and

c)   payments of any kind received as a consideration for the use of, or the right to use any industrial, commercial, or scientific equipment.

4.   The provisions of paragraphs 1 and 2 shall not apply if the beneficial owner of the royalties, being a resident of a Contracting State, carries on business in the other Contracting State through a permanent establishment situated therein and the right or property in respect of which the royalties are paid is effectively connected with such permanent establishment. In such case the provisions of Article 7 (Business Profits) shall apply.

5.   Royalties shall be deemed to arise in a Contracting State only to the extent that such royalties are payments made as consideration for the use of, or the right to use, property or rights described in paragraph 3 within that Contracting State.

6.   Where, by reason of a special relationship between the payer and the beneficial owner or between both of them and some other person, the amount of the royalties, having regard to the use, right, or information for which they are paid, exceeds the amount which would have been agreed upon by the payer and the beneficial owner in the absence of such relationship, the provisions of this Article shall apply only to the last-mentioned amount. In such case, the excess part of the payments shall remain taxable according to the laws of each Contracting State, due regard being had to the other provisions of the Convention.

Article 14
CAPITAL GAINS

1.   Gains derived by a resident of a Contracting State from the alienation of real property referred to in Article 6 (Income from Real Property) situated in the other Contracting State may be taxed in that other State.

2.   Gains derived by a resident of Poland that are attributable to the alienation of a United States real property interest may be taxed by the United States in accordance with its domestic law.

3.   Gains derived by a resident of the United States from the alienation of:

a)   shares, including rights to acquire shares, deriving more than 50 percent of their value directly or indirectly from real property situated in Poland; and

b)   an interest in a partnership or trust to the extent that the assets of the partnership or trust consist in aggregate more than 50 percent of real property situated in Poland, or of shares referred to subparagraph a);

may be taxed in Poland.

4.   Gains from the alienation of movable property forming part of the business property of a permanent establishment that an enterprise of a Contracting State has in the other Contracting State, including such gains from the alienation of such a permanent establishment (alone or with the whole enterprise), may be taxed in that other State.

5.   Gains derived by an enterprise of a Contracting State from the alienation of ships or aircraft operated in international traffic or movable property pertaining to the operation of such ships or aircraft shall be taxable only in that State.

6.   Gains derived by an enterprise of a Contracting State from the alienation of containers (including trailers, barges, and related equipment for the transport of containers) used for the transport of goods or merchandise in international traffic shall be taxable only in that Contracting State.

7.   Gains from the alienation of any property other than property referred to in paragraphs 1, 2, 3, 4, 5 and 6 of this Article shall be taxable only in the Contracting State of which the alienator is a resident.

Article 15
INCOME FROM EMPLOYMENT

1.   Subject to the provisions of Articles 16 (Directors' Fees), 18 (Pensions, Social Security, Annuities, Alimony, and Child Support) and 19 (Government Service), salaries, wages, and other similar remuneration derived by a resident of a Contracting State in respect of an employment shall be taxable only in that State unless the employment is exercised in the other Contracting State. If the employment is so exercised, such remuneration as is derived therefrom may be taxed in that other State.

2.   Notwithstanding the provisions of paragraph 1, remuneration derived by a resident of a Contracting State in respect of an employment exercised in the other Contracting State shall be taxable only in the first-mentioned State if:

a)   the recipient is present in the other State for a period or periods not exceeding in the aggregate 183 days in any twelve month period commencing or ending in the fiscal year concerned;

b)   the remuneration is paid by, or on behalf of, an employer who is not a resident of the other State; and

c)   the remuneration is not borne by a permanent establishment which the employer has in the other State.

3.   Notwithstanding the preceding provisions of this Article, remuneration described in paragraph 1 that is derived by a resident of a Contracting State in respect of an employment exercised aboard a ship or aircraft operated in international traffic as a member of the complement of the ship or aircraft shall be taxable only in that State.

Article 16
DIRECTORS' FEES

Directors' fees and other similar payments derived by a resident of a Contracting State in his capacity as a member of the board of directors of a company that is a resident of the other Contracting State may be taxed in that other Contracting State.

Article 17
ENTERTAINERS AND SPORTSMEN

1.   Income derived by a resident of a Contracting State as an entertainer, such as a theater, motion picture, radio, or television artiste, or a musician, or as a sportsman, from his personal activities as such exercised in the other Contracting State, which income would be exempt from tax in that other Contracting State under the provisions of Articles 7 (Business Profits) and 15 (Income from Employment) may be taxed in that other State, except where the amount of the gross receipts derived by such entertainer or sportsman, including expenses reimbursed to him or borne on his behalf, from such activities does not exceed twenty thousand United States dollars ($20,000) or its equivalent in Polish legal tender for the taxable year of the payment.

2.   Where income in respect of personal activities exercised by an entertainer or a sportsman in his capacity as such accrues not to the entertainer or sportsman himself but to another person, that income may, notwithstanding the provisions of Articles 7 and 15 of this Convention, be taxed in the Contracting State in which the activities of the entertainer or sportsman are exercised unless the contract pursuant to which the personal activities are performed allows that other person to designate the individual who is to perform the personal activities.

Article 18
PENSIONS, SOCIAL SECURITY, ANNUITIES,
ALIMONY, AND CHILD SUPPORT

1.   Pensions, annuities and other similar payments made to and beneficially owned by a resident of a Contracting State shall be taxable only in that State.

2.   Notwithstanding the provisions of paragraph 1, pensions and other similar payments arising in a Contracting State that, when received, would be exempt from taxation in that State if the beneficial owner were a resident thereof shall be exempt from taxation in the Contracting State of which the beneficial owner is a resident.

3.   Notwithstanding the provisions of paragraph 1, payments made by a Contracting State under the provisions of the social security or similar legislation of that State to a resident of the other Contracting State or to a citizen of the United States may be taxable only in the first-mentioned State.

4.   Where an individual who is a resident of one of the Contracting States is a member or beneficiary of, or participant in, a pension fund that is a resident of the other Contracting State, income earned by the pension fund may be taxed as income of that individual only when, and, subject to the provisions of paragraph 1, to the extent that, it is paid to, or for the benefit of, that individual from the pension fund (and not transferred to another pension fund in that other Contracting State).

5.   Alimony paid by a resident of a Contracting State to a resident of the other Contracting State and periodic payments for the support of a child made pursuant to a written separation agreement or a decree of divorce, separate maintenance, or compulsory support,

paid by a resident of a Contracting State to a resident of the other Contracting State, shall be exempt from tax in both Contracting States. The term "alimony" as used in this paragraph means periodic payments made pursuant to a written separation agreement or a decree of divorce, separate maintenance, or compulsory support, which payments are taxable to the recipient under the laws of the State of which he is a resident.

Article 19
GOVERNMENT SERVICE

1.   a)   Salaries, wages and other similar remuneration, paid by a Contracting State or a political subdivision or a local and governmental authority thereof to an individual in respect of services rendered to that State or subdivision or authority shall be taxable only in that State, subject to subparagraph b) of this paragraph.

    b)   However, such salaries, wages and other similar remuneration shall be taxable only in the other Contracting State if the services are rendered in that State and the individual is a resident of that State who:

        i)   is a national of that State; or

        ii)   did not become a resident of that State solely for the purpose of rendering the services.

2.   a)   Notwithstanding the provisions of paragraph 1 of Article 18 (Pensions, Social Security, Annuities, Alimony, and Child Support), any pensions, annuities and other similar payments paid by, or out of funds created by, a Contracting State or a political subdivision or a local and governmental authority thereof (other than a payment to which paragraph 2 of Article 18 applies) to an individual in respect of services rendered to that State or subdivision or authority shall be taxable only in that State.

    b)   However, such pensions, annuities and other similar payments shall be taxable only in the other Contracting State if the individual is a resident of, and a national of that State.

3.   The provisions of Articles 15 (Income from Employment), 16 (Director's Fees), 17 (Entertainers and Sportsmen) and 18 (Pensions, Social Security, Annuities, Alimony, and Child Support) of this Convention shall apply to salaries, wages, pensions and other similar

remuneration in respect of services rendered in connection with a business carried on by a Contracting State or a political subdivision or a local and governmental authority thereof.

Article 20
STUDENTS AND TRAINEES

1.   Payments, other than remuneration for personal services, received by a student, pupil or business trainee who is, or was immediately before visiting a Contracting State, a resident of the other Contracting State, and who is present in the first-mentioned State for the primary purpose of his education or training, shall not be taxed in that State, provided that such payments arise outside that State and are for the purpose of his maintenance, education or training. The exemption from tax provided by this paragraph shall apply to a business trainee only for a period of time not exceeding one year from the date the business trainee first arrives in the first-mentioned Contracting State for the purpose of training.

2.   A student, pupil or business trainee within the meaning of paragraph 1 shall be exempt from tax by the Contracting State in which the individual is temporarily present with respect to income from personal services in an aggregate amount equal to $9,000 or its equivalent in Polish legal tender annually.

3.   For purposes of this Article, a business trainee is an individual:

   a)   who is temporarily in a Contracting State for the purpose of securing training required to qualify the individual to practice a profession or professional specialty; or

   b)   who is temporarily in a Contracting State as an employee of, or under contract with, a resident of the other Contracting State, for the primary purpose of acquiring technical, professional, or business experience from a person other than that resident of the other Contracting State (or a person related to such resident of the other Contracting State).

Article 21
OTHER INCOME

1.   Items of income received by a resident of a Contracting State that are beneficially owned by a resident of that State, wherever arising, not dealt with in the foregoing Articles of this Convention shall be taxable only in that State.

2.   The provisions of paragraph 1 shall not apply to income, other than income from real property as defined in paragraph 2 of Article 6 (Income from Real Property), if the recipient of such income, being a resident of a Contracting State, carries on business in the other Contracting State through a permanent establishment situated therein and the right or property in respect of which the income is paid is effectively connected with such permanent establishment. In such case the provisions of Article 7 (Business Profits) shall apply.

Article 22
LIMITATION ON BENEFITS

1.   Except as otherwise provided in this Article, a resident of a Contracting State shall not be entitled to the benefits of this Convention otherwise accorded to residents of a Contracting State unless such resident is a "qualified person" as defined in paragraph 2.

2.   A resident of a Contracting State shall be a qualified person for a taxable year if the resident is:

    a)   an individual;

    b)   a Contracting State, or a political subdivision or local authority thereof, or an agency or instrumentality of that State, subdivision or authority;

    c)   a company, if:

        i)   the principal class of its shares (and any disproportionate class of shares) is regularly traded on one or more recognized stock exchanges, and either:

            A)   its principal class of shares is primarily traded on one or more recognized stock exchanges located in the Contracting State of which the company is a resident (or, in the case of a company resident in

Poland, on a recognized stock exchange located within the European Union or in any other European Free Trade Association (EFTA) state or, in the case of a company resident in the United States, on a recognized stock exchange located in another state that is a party to the North American Free Trade Agreement (NAFTA)); or

B) the company's primary place of management and control is in the Contracting State of which it is a resident; or

ii) at least 50 percent of the aggregate voting power and value of the shares (and at least 50 percent of any disproportionate class of shares) in the company is owned directly or indirectly by five or fewer companies entitled to benefits under clause i) of this subparagraph, provided that, in the case of indirect ownership, each intermediate owner is a resident of either Contracting State;

d) a person described in paragraph 2 of Article 4 (Resident), provided that, in the case of a person described in subparagraph a) of that paragraph, more than 50 percent of the person's beneficiaries, members or participants are individuals resident in either Contracting State; or

e) a person other than an individual, if:

i) on at least half the days of the taxable year, persons who are residents of that Contracting State and that are entitled to the benefits of this Convention under subparagraph a), subparagraph b), clause i) of subparagraph c), or subparagraph d) of this paragraph own, directly or indirectly, shares or other beneficial interests representing at least 50 percent of the aggregate voting power and value (and at least 50 percent of any disproportionate class of shares) of the person, provided that, in the case of indirect ownership, each intermediate owner is a resident of that Contracting State, and

ii) less than 50 percent of the person's gross income for the taxable year, as determined in the person's State of residence, is paid or accrued, directly or indirectly, to persons who are not residents of either Contracting State entitled to the benefits of this Convention under subparagraph a), subparagraph b), clause i) of subparagraph c), or subparagraph d) of this paragraph in the form of payments that are deductible for purposes of the taxes covered by this Convention in the person's State of residence (but not including arm's length payments in the ordinary course of business for services or tangible property).

3.　　Notwithstanding that a company that is a resident of a Contracting State may not be a qualified person, it shall be entitled to all the benefits of this Convention otherwise accorded to residents of a Contracting State with respect to an item of income if it satisfies any other specified conditions for the obtaining of such benefits and:

a)　　at least 95 percent of the aggregate voting power and value of its shares (and at least 50 percent of any disproportionate class of shares) is owned, directly or indirectly, by seven or fewer persons who are equivalent beneficiaries; and

b)　　less than 50 percent of the company's gross income, as determined in the company's State of residence, for the taxable year is paid or accrued, directly or indirectly, to persons who are not equivalent beneficiaries, in the form of payments that are deductible for purposes of the taxes covered by this Convention in the company's State of residence (but not including arm's length payments in the ordinary course of business for services or tangible property).

4.　　a)　　A resident of a Contracting State will be entitled to benefits of the Convention with respect to an item of income derived from the other Contracting State, regardless of whether the resident is a qualified person, if the resident is engaged in the active conduct of a trade or business in the first-mentioned State (other than the business of making or managing investments for the resident's own account, unless these activities are banking, insurance or securities activities carried on by a bank, insurance company or registered securities dealer), and the income derived from the other Contracting State is derived in connection with, or is incidental to, that trade or business.

b)　　If a resident of a Contracting State derives an item of income from a trade or business activity conducted by that resident in the other Contracting State, or derives an item of income arising in the other Contracting State from a related person, the conditions described in subparagraph a) shall be considered to be satisfied with respect to such item only if the trade or business activity carried on by the resident in the first-mentioned Contracting State is substantial in relation to the trade or business activity carried on by the resident or related person in the other Contracting State. Whether a trade or business activity is substantial for the purposes of this paragraph will be determined based on all the facts and circumstances.

c)   For purposes of applying this paragraph, activities conducted by persons connected to a person shall be deemed to be conducted by such person. A person shall be connected to another if one possesses at least 50 percent of the beneficial interest in the other (or, in the case of a company, at least 50 percent of the aggregate voting power and value of the company's shares or of the beneficial equity interest in the company) or another person possesses at least 50 percent of the beneficial interest (or, in the case of a company, at least 50 percent of the aggregate voting power and value of the company's shares or of the beneficial equity interest in the company) in each person. In any case, a person shall be considered to be connected to another if, based on all the relevant facts and circumstances, one has control of the other or both are under the control of the same person or persons.

5.   A person that is a resident of a Contracting State shall also be entitled to all the benefits of this Convention otherwise accorded to residents of a State if that person functions as a headquarters company for a multinational corporate group and that resident satisfies any specified conditions for the obtaining of such benefits other than those of this Article. A person shall be considered a headquarters company for this purpose only if:

a)   it provides a substantial portion of the overall supervision and administration of the group, which may include, but cannot be principally, group financing;

b)   the corporate group consists of corporations resident in, and engaged in an active business in, at least five countries, and the business activities carried on in each of the five countries (or five groupings of countries) generate at least 10 percent of the gross income of the group;

c)   the business activities carried on in any one country other than the Contracting State of residence of the headquarters company generate less than 50 percent of the gross income of the group;

d)   no more than 25 percent of its gross income is derived from the other Contracting State;

e)   it has, and exercises, independent discretionary authority to carry out the functions referred to in subparagraph a);

f)   it is subject to the same income taxation rules in its country of residence as persons described in paragraph 4; and

g)   the income derived in the other Contracting State either is derived in connection with, or is incidental to, the active business referred to in subparagraph b).

If the gross income requirements of subparagraphs b), c), or d) of this paragraph are not fulfilled, they will be deemed to be fulfilled if the required ratios are met when averaging the gross income of the preceding four years.

6.   Notwithstanding the preceding provisions of this Article, where an enterprise of a Contracting State derives income from the other Contracting State, and that income is attributable to a permanent establishment which that enterprise has in a third state, the tax benefits that would otherwise apply under the other provisions of the Convention will not apply to that income if the profits of that permanent establishment are subject to a combined aggregate effective rate of tax in the first-mentioned Contracting State and third state that is less than 60 percent of the general rate of company tax applicable in the first-mentioned Contracting State. Any dividends, interest or royalties to which the provisions of this paragraph apply shall be subject to tax in the other Contracting State at a rate that shall not exceed 15 percent of the gross amount thereof. Any other income to which the provisions of this paragraph apply shall be subject to tax under the provisions of the domestic law of the other Contracting State, notwithstanding any other provision of the Convention. The provisions of this paragraph shall not apply if:

a)   in the case of royalties, the royalties are received as compensation for the use of, or the right to use, intangible property produced or developed by the permanent establishment itself; or

b)   in the case of any other income, the income derived from the other Contracting State is derived in connection with, or is incidental to, the active conduct of a trade or business carried on by the permanent establishment in the third state (other than the business of making, managing or simply holding investments for the enterprise's own account, unless these activities are securities activities carried on by a registered securities dealer).

7.   If a resident of a Contracting State is neither a qualified person pursuant to the provisions of paragraph 2 nor entitled to benefits with respect to an item of income under paragraph 3 of this Article the competent authority of the other Contracting State may,

nevertheless, grant the benefits of this Convention, or benefits with respect to a specific item of income, if it determines that the establishment, acquisition or maintenance of such person and the conduct of its operations did not have as one of its principal purposes the obtaining of benefits under this Convention. The competent authority of the State in which the income arises will consult with the competent authority of the other State before denying the benefits of the Convention under this paragraph.

8.   For purposes of this Article:

    a)   the term "recognized stock exchange" means:

        i)   the NASDAQ System owned by the National Association of Securities Dealers, Inc. and any stock exchange registered with the U.S. Securities and Exchange Commission as a national securities exchange under the U.S. Securities Exchange Act of 1934;

        ii)   the Warsaw Stock Exchange;

        iii)   the stock exchanges of Amsterdam, Brussels, Budapest, Frankfurt, London, Mexico City, Montreal, Paris, Toronto, Vienna and Zurich;

        iv)   any other stock exchange agreed upon by the competent authorities;

    b)   the term "principal class of shares" means the ordinary or common shares of the company, provided that such class of shares represents the majority of the voting power and value of the company. If no single class of ordinary or common shares represents the majority of the aggregate voting power and value of the company, the "principal class of shares" are those classes that in the aggregate represent a majority of the aggregate voting power and value of the company;

    c)   the term "disproportionate class of shares" means any class of shares of a company resident in one of the Contracting States that entitles the shareholder to disproportionately higher participation, through dividends, redemption payments or otherwise, in the earnings generated in the other State by particular assets or activities of the company;

    d)   the shares of a company are "primarily traded" if the number of shares in the company's principal class of shares that are traded during the taxable year on all recognized stock exchanges in the Contracting State of which the company is a resident (or, in the case of a company resident in Poland, on a recognized stock exchange located within the European Union or in any other European Free Trade Association (EFTA) state or, in the case of a company resident in the United States, on a recognized stock exchange located in another state that is a party to the North American Free Trade Agreement (NAFTA)) exceeds the number of shares in the company's principal class of shares that are traded during that year on established securities markets in any other single foreign country;

e)   a company's "primary place of management and control" will be in the Contracting State of which it is a resident only if executive officers and senior management employees exercise day-to-day responsibility for more of the strategic, financial and operational policy decision making for the company (including its direct and indirect subsidiaries) in that State than in any other state and the staff of such persons conduct more of the day-to-day activities necessary for preparing and making those decisions in that State than in any other state;

f)   the term "equivalent beneficiary" means a resident of a member state of the European Union or of any other European Free Trade Association (EFTA) state or of a party to the North American Free Trade Agreement (NAFTA), but only if that resident:

i)   A)   would be entitled to all the benefits of a comprehensive convention for the avoidance of double taxation between any member state of the European Union or any other European Free Trade Association (EFTA) state or any party to the North American Free Trade Agreement (NAFTA) and the State from which the benefits of this Convention are claimed under provisions analogous to subparagraph a), b), clause i) of subparagraph c) or subparagraph d) of paragraph 2 of this Article, provided that if such convention does not contain a comprehensive limitation on benefits article, the person would be entitled to the benefits of this Convention by reason of subparagraph a), b), clause i) of subparagraph c) or subparagraph d) of paragraph 2 of this Article if such person were a resident of one of the States under Article 4 of this Convention; and

B)   with respect to income referred to in Article 10 (Dividends), 11 (Interest) or 13 (Royalties) of this Convention, would be entitled under such convention to a rate of tax with respect to the particular class of income for which benefits are being claimed under this Convention that is at least as low as the rate applicable under this Convention; or

ii)   is a resident of a Contracting State that is entitled to the benefits of this Convention by reason of subparagraph a), b), clause i) of subparagraph c) or subparagraph d) of paragraph 2 of this Article; and

g)   with respect to dividends, interest or royalties arising in Poland and beneficially owned by a company that is a resident of the United States, a company that is a resident of a member state of the European Union will be treated as satisfying the requirements of subparagraph f) i) B) of this paragraph for purposes of determining whether such United States resident is entitled to benefits under paragraph 3 if a payment of dividends, interest or royalties arising in Poland and paid directly to such resident of a member state of the European Union would have been exempt from tax pursuant to any directive of the European Union, notwithstanding that the income tax convention between Poland and that other member state of the European Union would provide for a higher rate of tax with respect to such payment than the rate of tax applicable to such United States company under Article 10, 11 or 13 of this Convention.

Article 23
ELIMINATION OF DOUBLE TAXATION

1.   In the case of Poland, double taxation shall be avoided as follows:

a)   Where a resident of Poland derives income which, in accordance with the provisions of this Convention may be taxed in the United States, Poland shall, subject to the provisions of subparagraph b) of this paragraph exempt such income from tax.

b)   Where a resident of Poland derives income or capital gains which, in accordance with the provisions of Articles 10 (Dividends), 11 (Interest), 13 (Royalties), 14 (Capital Gains) or 21 (Other Income) may be taxed in the United States, Poland shall allow as a deduction from the tax on the income or capital gains of that resident an amount equal to the tax paid in the United States. Such deduction shall not, however, exceed that part of the tax, as computed before the deduction is given, which is attributable to such income or capital gains derived from the United States.

c)   Where in accordance with any provision of this Convention, income derived by a resident of Poland is exempt from tax in Poland, Poland may nevertheless, in calculating the amount of tax on the remaining income of such resident, take into account the exempted income.

2.   In accordance with the provisions and subject to the limitations of the law of the United States (as it may be amended from time to time without changing the general principle hereof), the United States shall allow to a resident or citizen of the United States as a credit against the United States tax on income applicable to residents and citizens:

a)   the income tax paid or accrued to Poland by or on behalf of such resident or citizen; and

b)   in the case of a United States company owning at least 10 percent of the voting stock of a company that is a resident of Poland and from which the United States company receives dividends, the income tax paid or accrued to Poland by or on behalf of the payer with respect to the profits out of which the dividends are paid.

For the purposes of this paragraph, the taxes referred to in paragraphs 3 a) and 4 of Article 2 (Taxes Covered) shall be considered income taxes.

3.   For the purposes of applying paragraph 2 of this Article, an item of gross income, as determined under the laws of the United States, derived by a resident of the United States that, under this Convention, may be taxed in Poland shall be deemed to be income from sources in Poland.

4.   Where a United States citizen is a resident of Poland:

a)   with respect to items of income that under the provisions of this Convention are exempt from United States tax or that are subject to a reduced rate of United States tax when derived by a resident of Poland who is not a United States citizen, Poland shall allow as a credit against Polish tax, only the tax paid, if any, that the United States may impose under the provisions of this Convention, other than taxes that may be imposed solely by reason of citizenship under paragraph 4 of Article 1 (General Scope);

b)   for purposes of applying paragraph 2 to compute United States tax on those items of income referred to in subparagraph a), the United States shall allow as a credit against United States tax the income tax paid to Poland after the credit referred to in subparagraph a); the credit so allowed shall not reduce the portion of the United States tax that is creditable against the Polish tax in accordance with subparagraph a); and

c)   for the exclusive purpose of relieving double taxation in the United States under subparagraph b), items of income referred to in subparagraph a) shall be deemed to arise in Poland to the extent necessary to avoid double taxation of such income under subparagraph b).

5.   Where an individual, upon ceasing to be a resident of one of the Contracting States, is treated under the taxation law of that State as having alienated any property for its fair market value and is taxed in that State by reason thereof, the individual may elect to be treated for purposes of taxation in the other Contracting State as if the individual had, immediately before ceasing to be a resident of the first-mentioned State, alienated and reacquired such property for an amount equal to its fair market value at such time.

Article 24
NON-DISCRIMINATION

1.   Nationals of a Contracting State shall not be subjected in the other Contracting State to any taxation or any requirement connected therewith that is other or more burdensome than the taxation and connected requirements to which nationals of that other State in the same circumstances, in particular with respect to taxation on worldwide income, are or may be subjected. This provision shall also apply to persons who are not residents of one or both of the Contracting States.

2.   The taxation on a permanent establishment that an enterprise of a Contracting State has in the other Contracting State shall not be less favorably levied in that other State than the taxation levied on enterprises of that other State carrying on the same activities.

3.   The provisions of paragraphs 1 and 2 shall not be construed as obliging a Contracting State to grant to residents of the other Contracting State any personal allowances, reliefs, and reductions for taxation purposes on account of civil status or family responsibilities that it grants to its own residents.

4.   Except where the provisions of paragraph 1 of Article 9 (Associated Enterprises), paragraph 8 of Article 11 (Interest), or paragraph 6 of Article 13 (Royalties) apply, interest, royalties, and other disbursements paid by a resident of a Contracting State to a resident of the other Contracting State shall, for the purpose of determining the taxable profits of the first-mentioned resident, be deductible under the same conditions as if they had been paid to a resident of the first-mentioned State. Similarly, any debts of a resident of a Contracting State to a resident of the other Contracting State shall, for the purpose of determining the taxable capital of the first-mentioned resident, be deductible under the same conditions as if they had been contracted to a resident of the first-mentioned State.

5.   Enterprises of a Contracting State, the capital of which is wholly or partly owned or controlled, directly or indirectly, by one or more residents of the other Contracting State, shall not be subjected in the first-mentioned State to any taxation or any requirement connected therewith that is more burdensome than the taxation and connected requirements to which other similar enterprises of the first-mentioned State are or may be subjected.

6.   Nothing in this Article shall be construed as preventing either Contracting State from imposing a tax as described in paragraph 1 of Article 12 (Branch Profits).

7.   The provisions of this Article shall, notwithstanding the provisions of Article 2 (Taxes Covered), apply to taxes of every kind and description imposed by a Contracting State or a political subdivision or local authority thereof.

Article 25
MUTUAL AGREEMENT PROCEDURE

1.   Where a person considers that the actions of one or both of the Contracting States result or will result for such person in taxation not in accordance with the provisions of this Convention, it may, irrespective of the remedies provided by the domestic law of those States, and the time limits prescribed in such laws for presenting claims for refund, present its case to the competent authority of the Contracting State of which he is a resident or, if his case comes under paragraph 1 of Article 24, to that of the Contracting State of which he is a national. The case must be presented within three years from the first notification of the action resulting in taxation not in accordance with the provisions of this Convention.

2.   The competent authority shall endeavor, if the objection appears to it to be justified and if it is not itself able to arrive at a satisfactory solution, to resolve the case by mutual agreement with the competent authority of the other Contracting State, with a view to the

avoidance of taxation which is not in accordance with the Convention. Any agreement reached shall be implemented notwithstanding any time limits or other procedural limitations in the domestic law of the Contracting States.

3.   The competent authorities of the Contracting States shall endeavor to resolve by mutual agreement any difficulties or doubts arising as to the interpretation or application of the Convention. They also may consult together for the elimination of double taxation in cases not provided for in the Convention.

4.   The competent authorities of the Contracting States may communicate with each other directly, including through a joint commission consisting of themselves or their representatives, for the purpose of reaching an agreement in the sense of the preceding paragraphs.

Article 26
EXCHANGE OF INFORMATION

1.   The competent authorities of the Contracting States shall exchange such information as is foreseeably relevant for carrying out the provisions of this Convention or to the administration or enforcement of the domestic laws of the Contracting States concerning taxes of every kind and description imposed by a Contracting State, insofar as the taxation thereunder is not contrary to the Convention, including information relating to the assessment or collection of, the enforcement or prosecution in respect of, or the determination of appeals in relation to, such taxes. The exchange of information is not restricted by paragraph 1 of Article 1 (General Scope) or Article 2 (Taxes Covered).

2.   Any information received under this Article by a Contracting State shall be treated as secret in the same manner as information obtained under the domestic laws of that State and shall be disclosed only to persons or authorities (including courts and administrative bodies) involved with the assessment, or collection of, or administration of, the enforcement or prosecution in respect of, or the determination of appeals in relation to, the taxes referred to in paragraph 1, or the oversight of such functions. Such persons or authorities shall use the information only for such purposes. They may disclose the information in public court proceedings or in judicial decisions.

3.   In no case shall the provisions of the preceding paragraphs be construed so as to impose on a Contracting State the obligation:

a)   to carry out administrative measures at variance with the laws and administrative practice of that or of the other Contracting State;

b)   to supply information that is not obtainable under the laws or in the normal course of the administration of that or of the other Contracting State;

c)   to supply information that would disclose any trade, business, industrial, commercial, or professional secret or trade process, or information the disclosure of which would be contrary to public policy (ordre public).

4.   If information is requested by a Contracting State in accordance with this Article, the other Contracting State shall use its information gathering measures to obtain the requested information, even though that other State may not need such information for its own purposes. The obligation contained in the preceding sentence is subject to the limitations of paragraph 3 but in no case shall such limitation be construed to permit a Contracting State to decline to supply information because it has no domestic interest in such information.

5.   In no case shall the provisions of paragraph 3 be construed to permit a Contracting State to decline to supply information requested by the other Contracting State because the information is held by a bank, other financial institution, nominee or person acting in an agency or a fiduciary capacity or because it relates to ownership interests in a person.

6.   If specifically requested by the competent authority of a Contracting State, the competent authority of the other Contracting State shall provide information under this Article in the form of depositions of witnesses and authenticated copies of unedited original documents (including books, papers, statements, records, accounts, and writings).

7.   The competent authorities of the Contracting States may develop an agreement upon the mode of application of this Article, including agreement to ensure comparable levels of assistance to each of the Contracting States, but in no case will the lack of such agreement relieve a Contracting State of its obligations under this Article.

Article 27
MEMBERS OF DIPLOMATIC MISSIONS AND CONSULAR POSTS

Nothing in this Convention shall affect the fiscal privileges of members of diplomatic missions, permanent representations or consular posts under the general rules of international law or under the provisions of special agreements.

Article 28
ENTRY INTO FORCE

1.   This Convention shall be subject to ratification in accordance with the applicable procedures of each Contracting State. The Contracting States shall notify each other in writing, through diplomatic channels, that their respective applicable procedures have been satisfied.

2.   This Convention shall enter into force on the date of the later of the notifications referred to in paragraph 1, and its provisions shall have effect:

   a)   in respect of taxes withheld at source, for amounts paid or credited on or after the first day of the second month next following the date on which the Convention enters into force; and

   b)   in respect of other taxes, for taxable periods beginning on or after the first day of January next following the date on which the Convention enters into force.

3.   The Convention between the Government of the United States of America and the Government of the Polish People's Republic for the Avoidance of Double Taxation and the Prevention of Fiscal Evasion with Respect to Taxes on Income signed at Washington on 8th of October 1974 (hereinafter referred to as "the 1974 convention") shall cease to have effect in relation to any tax from the date upon which this Convention has effect in respect of such tax in accordance with the provisions of paragraph 2 of this Article. The 1974 convention shall terminate on the last date on which it has effect in relation to any tax in accordance with the foregoing provisions of this paragraph.

4.   Notwithstanding the entry into force of this Convention, an individual who was entitled to benefits of Article 17 (Teachers), Article 18 (Students and Trainees) or Article 19 (Government Functions) of the 1974 convention at the time of the entry into force of this Convention shall continue to be entitled to such benefits until such time as the individual would cease to be entitled to such benefits if the 1974 convention remained in force.

Article 29
TERMINATION

This Convention shall remain in force until terminated by one of the Contracting States. Either Contracting State may terminate the Convention by giving notice of termination to the other Contracting State through diplomatic channels on or before the thirtieth day of June in any calendar year beginning after the year in which the Convention enters into force. In such event, the Convention shall cease to have effect:

a) in respect of taxes withheld at source, for amounts paid or credited on or after the first day of January of the calendar year next following the date on which the notice is given; and

b) in respect of other taxes, for taxable periods beginning on or after the first day of January of the calendar year next following the date on which the notice is given.

IN WITNESS WHEREOF, the undersigned, being duly authorized thereto by their respective Governments, have signed this Convention.

DONE at Warsaw, in duplicate, in the English and Polish languages, both texts being equally authentic, this thirteenth day of February, 2013.

FOR THE UNITED STATES OF AMERICA: FOR THE REPUBLIC OF POLAND:

www.ingramcontent.com/pod-product-compliance
Lightning Source LLC
Chambersburg PA
CBHW060442290526
45793CB00002B/544